MW01713906

Disney's

# THE NEW ADVENTURES OF WINNIE the POOH

# Windswept Away

Amanda

Love,
Grandma
+
Grandpa

For St. Valentine's Day
1991

Twin Books

It was a windy day in the Hundred-Acre Wood. Piglet was on his way to visit Rabbit when he got swept up by the wind.

It lifted him up with a gust and let him down gently with a sigh. It spun him around like a top and blew him right into a bird's nest.

It was so windy that Winnie the Pooh ran to shut his window—but before he could shut it, Piglet blew right through and wound up inside Pooh's potbelly stove.

HUN

MR SANDERZ
ALSO RING

Poor Piglet blew right up the stovepipe to the roof of Pooh's house... and off he went again, blowing swiftly through the Hundred-Acre Wood towards Rabbit's house.

"I do hope Rabbit is in the mood for visitors," Piglet said.

Rabbit sat happily in front of his fireplace. "There's nothing cozier than the wind outside and me warm and comfortable inside," he said.

Then he heard a knock at his door and opened it.

"Is there something I can do for you?" he asked.

"Yes—*HELP!*" cried Piglet as the wind blew him in.

“Come down here at once!” Rabbit ordered, as he caught his favorite teapot.

“If I could come down,” said Piglet, “I wouldn’t be up.”

And as suddenly as he blew into Rabbit’s house, Piglet blew out again.

Meanwhile, Tigger was eating lunch with Kanga and Roo. Roo saw Piglet fly up against the window.

"Look! There's a piglet on our window!" said Roo.

But before Tigger could turn, Piglet blew away. "I don't see any piglet," said Tigger.

Piglet was blowing towards his own house. "Oh, finally!" he cried. "Home, sweet home!"

He crashed through the door and into a pile of furniture. "I'm never going out into the wind again!" he declared.

The next day, Pooh, Rabbit, and Tigger visited Piglet to see if he was all right. They found Piglet hiding under his chair.

"It's too dangerous for such a very small animal to be out in such a very large wind," said Piglet.

"But ya can't stay under there forever, Piglet," said Tigger.

Pooh agreed with Tigger and said that the wind was nothing to fear. "In fact," Pooh said, "why don't we just open up this window?"

Pooh opened the window, and the wind blew Piglet right out from under his chair and swept him all around the room before Pooh could shut the window again.

Piglet ran back under the chair.

"This is more serious than I thought," said Pooh. "What we need is a plan to get Piglet out from under."

Pooh came up with an idea. He and Tigger and Rabbit went outside.

Pooh knocked on Piglet's door. "Telegram for Piglet!" he yelled.

Before opening the door, Piglet tied heavy bricks to his feet so that he wouldn't blow away. But as soon as he opened the door, the wind blew him away from the bricks, and he flew around the room like a leaf.

"We'll just have to try another approach," said Rabbit. He suggested that they visit Gopher.

When Pooh, Tigger, and Rabbit told Gopher about Piglet, Gopher came up with a plan. But he needed their help.

TRESPASSERS
WILL

Gopher showed Pooh, Tigger, and Rabbit how to dig a tunnel. The best way to get Piglet out of his house, Gopher thought, would be for him to go underground, where there was no wind.

After tunneling for a while, they stopped. "According to my precise calculations," said Gopher, "we're directly under Piglet's house." They began to dig straight up.

But Gopher had miscalculated. They dug up underneath a pond, which drained straight down on top of them!

Rabbit said, "Whatever we do next, I hope it's a little less . . . moist."

Later, wrapped in blankets and drinking hot chocolate, Pooh, Tigger, and Rabbit tried to get dry and warm.

"There's only one thing left to do," said Pooh. "Since Piglet's not coming out and we can't get him out, we'll just give him a Staying-Inside Party. It's like a Going-Away Party—only different."

The next day, everyone came to Piglet's Staying-Inside Party on the hill in front of Piglet's house. Pooh stopped inside to give Piglet a pinwheel as a gift and then joined the others outside.

Rabbit said, "I remember when we used to push Piglet on this swing. I wonder if he misses that."

As the sun set, Pooh said, “I remember when Piglet and I sat here watching the sunset. I wonder if he misses that.”

From his window, Piglet could hear what they had said. “I do miss that,” he said.

That night, after all of Piglet's friends went home, another windstorm raged through the Hundred-Acre Wood.

Piglet sighed when he saw that the wind was worse than before. Just then, he noticed Pooh trying to walk toward him. The wind was pushing Pooh right and left.

Suddenly a giant gust of wind blew Pooh end over end, until his scarf got snagged in a broken branch growing on the edge of the Hundred-Acre Cliff.

Dangling helplessly, Pooh watched in terror as his scarf began to unravel.

"Hang on, Pooh!" Piglet shouted.

The wind caught Piglet's pinwheel and blew Piglet right over to Pooh.

Suddenly, Pooh's scarf tore. Pooh began to fall.
"Q-quick! T-take my hand!" yelled Piglet.
"Why, thank you, Piglet," said Pooh.

The wind caught the pinwheel, and Pooh and Piglet glided gently downward to the grass at the bottom of the cliff.

"Piglet, though I was coming to save you from the wind, you used the wind to save me!" Pooh said. "But your staying-inside present is ruined."

Indeed, the wind had torn the pinwheel apart.

"I don't need a staying-inside present anymore," Piglet said. "Because I'm outside again."

Said Pooh, "I'm glad, Piglet. I'm very glad!"